Puppy Preschool

Puppy Preschool

Practical help and
advice for your puppy's
first year

MARIE TOSHACK

SMITHMARK

With thanks to my friends, local veterinarians and the highly experienced dog trainers who all lent their time and advice to the book.

The publishers would like to thank Belinda Carpenter and Pets Paradise of Eastgardens Pagewood, and Isabella Manfredi and "Saba" for their help and their puppies; and photographers Oliver Strewe and Ernie Kaltenbach.

This edition published in 1999 by SMITHMARK Publishers, a division of U.S. Media Holdings, Inc., 115 West 18th Street, New York, NY 10011.

SMITHMARK books are available for bulk purchase for sales promotion and premium use. For details write or call the manager of special sales, SMITHMARK Publishers, 115 West 18th Street, New York, NY 10011.

Produced by: Brewster Publishers Pty Ltd
PO Box 3231, Tamarama NSW 2026 Australia

ISBN: 0-7651-1030-X

Printed by South China Printing Co. (1988) Ltd, Hong Kong

10 9 8 7 6 5 4 3 2 1

Library of Congress Catalog Card Number: 98-61234

Contents

Eating, fighting, stealing socks and the baby's cuddly toys, digging up precious shrubs and peeing in the corner — it's a normal day in the life of a puppy.

All owners dream their puppy will be the perfect bundle of joy and energy—well-behaved, welcome wherever it goes, "house trained" overnight, will come running when called, will never jump up with muddy paws or slobber over visitors, and will never be a problem. A nice wish; but life, and puppy dogs, are a little more complicated than that.

If the owner can meet the puppy's requirements—give firm leadership from the day it comes home, care for it and train it—the puppy will respond with constant joy, loyalty and faithful companionship for life.

What sort of dog will my puppy grow into?

Little puppies are so cute that we seldom think of what lies ahead. Here is a check list to think about when purchasing your puppy.

- What will this gangly little fur-ball look like when its fully grown?
- Will it fit my needs? How will it fit in with my family?
- Do I want a big dog or small dog, a retriever or terrier, lap dog or guard dog?
- Purebred or a crossbred? Often the crossbreeds have strong constitutions and make devoted companions.
- Female or male?
- Do I want an allergy-free breed?
- Once it leaves its mother it is going to be totally reliant on me— will I be prepared for this?
- It is going to need house training, obedience training, love and affection, a good diet, regular exercise and grooming.
- Is it going to be an outside dog or an inside dog?
- Should it be neutered?
- Look for the best natured dog in the litter. A good guide for this is whether its mother is good-natured.
- Be careful choosing the weaker puppies from a litter, and the headstrong ones.

There are many ways to inspect different breeds. If you have fallen in love with a dog on television, check out the breed at a dog show. It may be quite different in real life. Find out from friends about their dogs; if you have small children ask questions about a puppy with a suitable temperament. Have a family conference and visit some kennels to take a closer look at promising breeds. Compare prices: a "must have" breed may also be a new import, still in limited supply, and very expensive.

Select a dog for your space, your time (grooming, exercise) and your budget (weekly food bills, kennel and equipment, occasional grooming, worm and external parasite treatment, registration, and veterinary fees). It is more important to pick a dog that is right for your family than to buy the latest "fashion accessory" breed.

Puppy psychology

Dogs are very social pack animals that can accept humans as substitution for their own species. Problems can arise when they are left alone all day. They can become bored and show other signs of distress such as digging the garden beds and barking. This not only upsets the owners, but often the neighbors too.

If puppies lack opportunities to socialize with humans (and other dogs) at an early age

this can lead to timidness, fear, poor behavior and even aggression.

Even in play do not teach or encourage a young puppy to be aggressive. This leads to problems and unpredictable behavior later in its life.

Pets should never be trained to attack. Dogs which are not aggressive can still attack because they feel fear when threatened or cornered, or when trying to exert their authority. Dogs can be excited by high pitched cries (children) or running (joggers) and attack. Dogs are by nature territorial and protect "their" property.

All dogs will bite people under certain conditions but the strong aggressive breeds—such as the pit bull terriers, rottweilers, dobermanns and German shepherds—can inflict terrible injuries, especially on small children and the elderly.

Many dog breeds are excellent and placid with children if parents have been careful owners and trained the dogs (and children) well. This writer, when aged two, was gently pulled out of a river by two working dogs on a farm; a faithful blue cattle dog and an Australian kelpie, both now "named" as breeds to avoid with small children.

Safe breeds

When it comes to children and dogs there are a few breeds that do come highly recommended. Golden retrievers, Cavalier King Charles spaniels, Whippets and Pugs are the highly recommended dog breeds for homes with young children under ten years of age. But there are many more breeds that are great for family pets. Even with recommended family-safe dog breeds, children should always be supervised by parents.

Golden retrievers have long coats and love the water. Big and strong, they are renown for their gentle tolerant nature which makes them excellent family dogs. They bond closely with owners, are very intelligent and love long walks.

Cavalier King Charles spaniels are always favorites with adults and children. Domesticated, small and affectionate, they are real indoor dogs.

Pugs have the unfortunate resemblance to a clenched fist with a tiny curl of a tail, but this belies their very friendly, docile nature. Being so small, they are very good with tiny children.

Whippets were once racing dogs. Resembling greyhounds, but smaller, they are affectionate, smart and rarely aggressive.

Airedale terriers are the biggest of the many terriers, like soft toys with a big beard around the face and legs. Big and boisterous, they are real extroverts and love people and kids.

Akita Inu is the national dog of Japan. While bred as hunting and guard dogs, these large powerful dogs have been used to "mind" children while parents work in the fields. Firm training is essential. They are loyal and intensely protective. Good with children.

Australian cattle dogs are strong-minded individuals, that will die in the cause of duty to guard their family, especially the children. Used to hard discipline and hard work in the paddocks of the outback, they need lots of exercise to use up their energy. Famous for being easily trained but will nip and bite if provoked and tormented. Cattle dogs dislike cats.

Australian silky terriers make good little watch dogs despite their tiny size. Very intelligent and excellent with children if taken into the home as puppies. Watch them with tiny children, with their tendency to leap up; easily excited by childish noises.

Basenjis are dogs that don't bark and seem ideal city dogs, though bred in Africa to hunt wild game. Obviously quiet around the house (they make only chortling or whining noises); they groom themselves like cats and are very protective and intelligent. Very loyal to children in the family.

Basset hounds are intelligent and see themselves as the important part of the family. Quiet with children. Head strong when following a scent, bassets need extra attention at training or they follow their stubborn streak. Will bark at strangers as well as at foxes or rabbits.

Cocker spaniels are not known for their great intellects but are greatly loved for their gentle fun-loving natures.

Dachshunds are devoted to their owners and stand-offish with strangers. The breed is intelligent and self-willed. They make good children's pets because they have lots of energy and training is not a problem.

Jack Russell terriers are brave and fun-loving; they are extremely loyal protecting their family. Smart with a mind of their own. Excellent with children.

Labradors were seemingly bred to be with children, as labs are protective of their young charges. They are used as guide dogs for the blind and pets as therapy, because of their gentle nature, but can be playful and lively with children. Friendly and intelligent dogs.

Maltese terriers are sweet tempered and loyal loving companions. Easy to train and adapt to households which are not too enthusiastic about daily exercise—a very short walk will keep the Maltese happy.

Poodles come in three sizes (toys, miniatures and standards) and all are bright and intelligent, with excellent personalities. They will learn tricks and do well in obedience classes. Happy dogs to live with and to train but, before you buy, make sure the mother is a happy dog. They do not shed and are regarded as allergy-free.

Schnauzers are very robust, square shaped dogs, with the big eyebrows and long bushy whiskers and moustache. Good family dogs but need to socialize with young children while still at the puppy stage.

Scottish terriers have the typical Celtic attitude—dour, fiery and faithful. True Scots, they are loyal to the last breath defending their owners and most are excellent with small children if they are used to them.

Pick of the litter

When you inspect a litter, look at and handle the mother (and the sire too, if he's still around). If the mother is friendly and well-behaved, there is every chance the puppies will inherit that temperament. If she appears even slightly aggressive, neurotic or nervy and is not the angelic disposition you expected, look elsewhere. Is the mother's size and coat exactly what you imagined the fully-grown dog to be like? The kennels should be clean and tidy if the puppies are to be healthy.

The puppies must be at least six to eight weeks old, have been weaned and ready to bond with people. Look for a puppy that is outgoing and happy at meeting and playful with newcomers. It should respond warmly to attention, and come when called by the breeder. Stubborn and strong-willed puppies can be difficult to train; they are highly intelligent but easily bored which leads them into mischief. Avoid a puppy which cringes or appears too timid as they can be the most difficult to train, and will require a great deal of patience and commitment.

A suitable puppy should be clean, warm and flea-free. Its tongue and gums should be pink and healthy looking. Check that the teeth and jaws line up. Eyes should be bright and never pink or have a discharge. Avoid puppies with smelly ears (signs of mites or ear infections). Don't pick thin or over fat puppies and reject puppies with a hernia-bulge in the navel, stomach or bottom. Never accept a puppy with signs of diarrhea or a runny nose. Make sure the coat is free of skin infections. Finally, make sure the legs are straight with no lumps or swollen joints.

Coming home

When you arrive home with the new puppy, give it time to become familiar with its new surroundings. This is its first time away from its mother and litter mates and, after the initial excitement, it will undoubtedly feel a little lost and forlorn.

Handle the young puppy gently. Lift it up, putting one hand under the rump and the other hand under its chest. Show children how to do this.

If you must pick it up by the scruff of the neck, the way the mother dog does, a hand under the hindquarters helps take the strain.

Food dishes, toys, a collar and bed for the puppy should be bought before bringing it home. The puppy will need supplementary feeding until it is four months old. The whole family should share in feeding, walking and playing with the new puppy so it doesn't become too attached to one member of the household or try to dominate the children.

A veterinary check should be made as soon as possible to confirm the puppy is healthy and to set up its course of vaccinations. Early veterinary visits, with lots of encouragement and praise, ensure the puppy gets used to being given pills, injections, having its temperature taken, and submitting to having various parts of its anatomy examined by strangers.

Nervous, frightened puppies that growl, snap and make a fuss in strange situations have to be dragged and pulled into the veterinary clinic, which is something both owner and veterinarian will want to avoid. By handling the puppy all over several times a day, including its hindquarters and tail, it should lose its fear of being touched and "bottom shyness" modesty when the vet takes its temperature or checks for anal gland problems.

Socializing

The human-to-dog bonding begins on Day one, as soon as you bring home your new puppy. Show it the new surroundings in a calm friendly manner. It must meet your family, your other pets, and your friends and their children. Encourage visitors to handle the puppy as much as possible after giving it a few days to settle in. Puppies need the mental and physical stimulation of human company in place of their mother and litter.

Don't allow young children to get the puppy over-excited and involve it in rough play or handling. Puppies tend to operate at full speed, then get suddenly very tired and collapse in a heap into a deep sleep. Children must quickly understand that the puppy needs undisturbed rest and sleep, just like they did when they were babies.

For the first few weeks the puppy must not mix with strange dogs which could be unhealthy or taken out on walks in parks or sidewalks where it could pick up diseases or infections. Dogs from outside the household can safely be introduced once the puppy has had all its vaccinations and begins to have daily walks. If you live on a busy road, introduce the puppy to the noise, or crowds of people gradually and calmly.

It is much easier to start teaching a puppy socially acceptable behavior immediately after you take it home than waiting six months or more for obedience classes when it has matured (and learned bad habits).

Responsible pet ownership includes regular handling—teaching the puppy to cope with people, loud noises, other dogs and cats, children and everyday life—while it learns basic obedience commands of "no, sit, stay, heel and come" which will make life easier for everyone.

Learning to lead

Before its first walk out on the street, the puppy must learn to lead. If it objects strongly and fights the leash attached to its new collar, try putting it on before feeding it and keep the meal on another side of the room. Hold the leash while the puppy goes over to the food and let it trail on the floor while it is eating. Repeat this over several meal times until the puppy stops fighting the collar and leash and begins associating it with its meal.

The puppy will probably have a temper tantrum when you first tie it up, but that is something it will have to get used to for emergencies, when it is the best way of restraining a puppy or dog.

The first short walks will be a slow and awkward stop-and-go pace as the puppy adjusts to this strange new "game."

Good manners

Animal behaviorists focus on "positive reinforcement" or rewards (such as small dog treats) when training puppies. Training should be fun for both owner and puppy while teaching the puppy some good manners.

Start with happy playing sessions, then introduce the day's first "lesson." Lavish lots of love and attention on the puppy and always use positive reinforcement (rewards), never punishment, when training.

The very first lesson for your puppy to learn is its name. Call the puppy using its name and reward it with lots of affection when it comes. If your puppy doesn't know its name teaching it will be very difficult.

Young puppies have short attention spans, so the early training sessions should not be more than 5 minutes. Repeat these several times a day. Always use the same word for the basic commands. Always use its name before each command ("Tigger, sit.") and speak in a firm, clear voice.

No: don't!

The most repeated word the puppy will hear for at least 12 months is "No." It will mean don't bite, don't bark, don't jump, don't go there. Use "No!" firmly, in a deep tone—and mean it. Follow it up with a command, such as "come here" or "sit" and when the puppy obeys, reward it.

Sit: sit down!

This is an important lesson for puppies and ensures the puppy's bottom is properly on the ground and the response is instantaneous. It can be best put into practice before meals, walks, grooming, play times and cuddles. Hold something tasty in your hand and gradually put it in front of the puppy's nose and raise it over its head. The puppy will lift its head to follow your hand and its bottom will rest on the ground. As soon as it sits, give the puppy the treat as a reward.

Next time you attempt the exercise say, "Sit," as the puppy's bottom touches the ground and give it the treat and a cuddle. Use the word often and keep rewarding it for obeying the command.

Another approach is to put the puppy on a leash. Walk together for a minute then stop, immediately tell the puppy to "sit." At the same time hold the puppy's head up using the leash and with a flat hand push down firmly on its rump to encourage it to sit. When it is sitting reward it with a good pat.

Not all puppies will catch on immediately. Keep trying until the puppy associates sitting down with rewards and knows the command to sit down every time.

Stay: don't move!

This is a good command to make sure the puppy does not run across the road when separated from the owner for example.

Use a sharp tone, coupled with a hand held out palm first. Ask the puppy to sit, take one step backwards, then quickly step forward and reward the puppy for not moving. Never move too far back in the beginning and always come back to reward and praise the puppy. If the puppy moves, you may have moved too far or left the puppy too long. Teach it to sit and stay. Then move on to using the "stay" command without rewards every time.

Never forget to say, "Come!" when the puppy is free to move off the spot. Then praise and cuddle the puppy.

Come: come here!

This is a good command because it can stop accidents happening. Training can begin on a long leash to ensure the puppy's attention. Never scold the puppy that answers the "Come!" command even if it was doing something wrong when it was called. Use an encouraging tone of voice and beckon the puppy with one hand.

Down! / Drop!

Give this command with a short, sharp voice and insist on an instant response, pointing to the ground with one hand. When the puppy is sitting, hold the food between your fingers and guide the puppy's nose to the floor. As soon as it is lying on the floor, give it the reward.

The puppy will learn to wait in this position.

Heel: come behind.

Learning to "heel" is a great discipline for a puppy and can keep it safe when crossing the road with its owner and when sudden problems occur.

- Put a light leash on the puppy and start walking.

- Let the puppy walk ahead of you but keep the leash relatively short.
- When it pulls tight, stop walking until the puppy stops pulling and the leash hangs loose; then start walking again.

The puppy will learn that you won't move until the leash is loose; but more importantly it will learn to walk at your pace.

Once owner and puppy have mastered the loose leash technique, it is time for the puppy to start learning to "heel"—that is, walking at your pace slightly behind and to the side of you.

Start off as before, but this time shorten the leash and hold it so the puppy is walking just slightly behind you. As it does say, "Heel," every few paces so puppy gets the message. When it gets it right, reward it with a pat and lavish praise.

It is a good idea to be consistent about what side the puppy is going heel to—your left or your right. Even small things like this can confuse it. Also change your direction frequently so the puppy gets the idea "wherever you go I shall follow."

Once the puppy is walking to heel on the leash, remove the leash and repeat the procedures so the puppy walks to heel unrestrained.

House training

"Is it house trained?" is the first question asked of breeders by inexperienced new owners—who may well imagine babies come toilet trained too. The young puppy will relieve itself every half hour to begin with. And every "accident" will set back its house training.

A concerted effort by the whole family in putting the puppy outside after every meal or after every sleep can dramatically hasten house training. Most puppies will be trained by 10 to 14 weeks, but it depends on the owner's time and commitment, rather like toilet training babies. Patience in building up a pattern of behavior is the key word.

The first thing the owner must decide is an area of the yard to set aside for the pup's elimination. The puppy has a natural instinct not to soil its own bed so take it straight to this area immediately after it wakes up and again after eating and drinking or after playing a vigorous game—the usual times it is most likely to make a mess. (The puppy must eat a well-balanced diet or it may suffer diarrhea which makes house training near impossible.)

At other times there are the usual warning signals—the puppy suddenly ignoring what it was doing and sniffing around the floor or becoming restless and running around in circles. Accidents usually occur on the carpet, behind a sofa or in an out-of-the-way corner of a room.

It can still be quite a wait outside (despite the initial urgency signs indoors) but praise the puppy when it does relieve itself. It is a good time to start rewarding the puppy too, with a small dog treat.

As an owner you must be patient. If you do catch the puppy "in the act," say "No!" loudly and firmly, clap your hands and carry it outside immediately (even if it is too late) for it to make the association with its own toilet area.

Never resort to "rubbing the puppy's nose in it" before it is house trained or punishing a puppy for accidents while it has been shut inside. Dogs can't reason and the puppy won't know why it is being punished in retrospect because it simply cannot connect making the mess with the owner's anger later on. It can even make the puppy find out-of-the-way places indoors for its toilet if the owner is always displeased with it.

If you come home and scold it, saying "Bad puppy!" do not assume it knows what you are talking about. The puppy looks guilty when you speak harshly because it is learning to associate those words with your displeasure. Animal behaviorists stress this makes a "bad association of punishment with the owner's homecoming."

Some owners scatter newspapers around the puppy's bed for it to use, but if it will not be confined inside all day it will only have to be trained not to use the newspapers in a few more weeks. Try not to confuse it.

At night take the puppy outside before going to bed, and again first thing in the morning. If you are a light sleeper and can muster the enthusiasm, take the puppy outside at other times during the night.

During the day, the puppy can be left outside if its bedding, food and water is always sheltered and it has a short run. The puppy won't relieve itself on the bedding and gets used to using the grass or a patch of sand at the end of its "run" as a place for elimination.

If someone is home during the day, the puppy should be close enough to hear what is going on indoors and should have a member of the family or a neighbor come along regularly with its meals and for company if it starts crying and barking. A little puppy left alone all day will become distressed.

Meal times

Puppies, like babies, need several meals a day—breakfast, lunch and dinner with a warm supper before bed. Ask the breeder what it was being fed. They will often recommend continuing with the diet the puppy has become used to. As a rough guide a young puppy's meals could be as follows:

Breakfast: baby cereal and milk

Lunch: a commercial puppy food, softened with water

Dinner: ground chicken or beef, mashed vegetables and (overcooked) rice with a sprinkling of a vitamin supplement

Supper: tepid milk

Make sure the puppy *always* has a bowl of fresh water.

As it grows, the puppy can also eat suitable table scraps and dried foods. It needs a varied diet consisting of natural foods as well as commercial pet brands (avoid using a single brand or product as the puppy may refuse to eat anything else). Meat should not

exceed 25 percent of the puppy's total diet. The more varied the diet, the better it is for the puppy.

If any foods make it sick or give it diarrhea, remove those foods from its diet and try again in a week or more. Veterinary advice must be sought if the stomach upset continues for more than 24 hours.

As it grows, the midday meal can be dropped from the puppy's diet. By the time it is six months old, it can be restricted to two meals a day and may have its main meal in the evening.

Feeding the young dog after everyone else has had their meal in the evening helps to establish in the puppy's mind, that you and the rest of the family are the "boss" dogs.

To avoid problems with begging set a rule that food is never given between meals and if it is, then it is served to the dog in it's dish, not from your hand. Never ever offer the puppy pieces of food from your dinner table or you will forever have a begging dog. Offering little snacks all through the day will teach your puppy that you are a never ending source of food and the puppy will follow you around in the hope of more treats.

Bad eating habits lead to obesity and dogs, like humans, suffer from health problems when they are overweight.

A good night's sleep

The new puppy should come home to its own basket or box with warm bedding (which can be washed). Its first bed can be a cut-down carton which needs to be big enough to allow the puppy to comfortably turn around and curl up or lie flat. It should be put somewhere warm and quiet and free of drafts. If it must be on a cold concrete floor in a bathroom or laundry, put an electric heating pad under the box.

Owners should not let the puppy sleep on the bed "just for the first night" or it will be there for life. Besides, it won't be house trained yet.

Show the puppy its new bed. For the first week a warm bed for the puppy to snuggle into, a night light, and ticking clock (to sound like its mother's heart beat) may help the puppy settle in and stop it whimpering and crying at night. A softly-playing radio may also make it feel less abandoned. Put in some soft puppy toys to chew. A den-like place to sleep makes the puppy feel secure and keeps it from getting underfoot.

Don't rush out too soon to comfort the puppy when it cries during the night (unless you are taking it outside to relieve itself). This will only prolong the settling in period.

The young puppy should sleep for long periods. Let it wake naturally. During the day, it will play, then sleep for an hour or so. Rest in these early weeks is essential for the development of a healthy body and good temperament. If the puppy gets over-excited playing, lift it back into its bed and keep it quiet.

When older, the puppy can move onto a washable trampoline bed which keeps it off the floor. Some dogs love beanbags to sleep on. If it is to live outside, the puppy can sleep in a kennel or on its trampoline bed in the garage or back porch.

Kennels, if they are big enough, give dogs good shelter from the elements but severely restrict their line of vision; dogs like to keep a good look-out on all that is going on around their territory.

Bath time

Puppies are like small boys, they hate baths. When they hear the word "bath" they will take off under a bed or under the house and won't be seen until they think the danger has long passed.

Keep the puppy confined in a room or tied up while you prepare the bath of tepid water. Mothers know to test with their elbow to make sure the water is not too hot. The puppy will need to have its collar on with a short leash to prevent it from leaping out of the bath as soon as you lift it in. Owners of unruly puppies may need to put on their swim suits.

For a long or floppy-eared puppy, try to avoid getting water in its ears and make sure the inside of its ears are wiped dry to guard against infections. This is also the time to wipe any discharges from around the puppy's eyes using cotton tips or moistened cotton balls. Long-haired toy breeds may need their long forehead hair tied back with a plastic hair clip or rubber band to keep it out of the eyes.

It is best to consult your local veterinarian about puppy shampoos and flea treatments. Make sure to rinse shampoos away from the puppy's eyes—a flexible hand-held shower hose is very useful.

By the end of bathing, the puppy will most likely make a sudden leap out of the bath and shake itself vigorously all over the owner. Always keep the puppy on a leash and don't allow it to become over-excited or you will get as wet as the puppy.

To dry the puppy, towel it, take it out for a quick run on a leash, or tie it up on clean grass in the sun—otherwise it will immediately roll in the nearest dirt to dry itself. Always wash the puppy early enough for it to dry in the heat of the day. For a long-haired dog or in cold weather, a hand-held hair dryer can be used to quickly dry the coat.

There is also the more costly alternative of puppy grooming parlors if washing and grooming your pet is too time consuming.

For a large dog, backyard bathing in an old tub or bucket of warm water with a large car sponge is just as efficient. Wet the dog all over, then put a line of dog shampoo down its back and work the suds in with the sponge. Rinse thoroughly, using either a bucket of clean, warm water or the garden hose.

Grooming

A lot of popular breeds require regular grooming. To get the puppy used to the idea of being groomed, brush the puppy's coat once a day for at least 5 minutes. The breeder, a grooming parlor, vet or pet shop will be able to advise on the type of brush required.

Sit the puppy up on a table or bench so that it is at a comfortable height and can not easily escape. The puppy should be taught to sit and stand quietly while being brushed. Once the puppy learns to be cooperative, grooming can be less often—once a week or as needed.

Pills and medicines

When it comes to giving pills, don't encourage the dogs-behaving-badly attitude. Assert yourself; you are the owner and you must take charge. Learn to give a pill properly. "Hiding" a pill in a piece of meat takes most dogs one second to sniff out and ignore or spit out.

Copy your veterinarian and sit the dog up on a table or bench. If you try to give the medicine at floor level, the dog has the distinct physical advantage and will probably end up sitting on you. In the beginning, get someone to sit behind it and firmly hold the dog around the shoulders.

- Face the dog and hold onto its muzzle.
- Push its cheeks open between the big fang teeth with one hand, then slip your left thumb in and tickle the roof of the mouth. This makes the dog open its mouth.
- Hold the pill between thumb and second finger of your other hand.
- Put it in the dog's mouth and push the pill down to the very back of the tongue at lightning speed. Keep the finger between the fang teeth, not across them, to avoid an accidental bite.
- Stroke the dog's throat which should make it swallow the pill.

Some cunning dogs will keep the pill in their throat until your attention is diverted, then get rid of it. Veterinarians push the pill right down the throat with an applicator, something you may need if you keep having problems.

Some dogs will shake their heads vigorously from side to side to prevent you from opening the mouth; others clench their teeth and refuse to open their jaws. Not many actually bite.

To give the puppy liquid medicine:

- Hold its muzzle and point the head up.
- Pull out a corner of the lip flap to form a pouch.
- Pour the mixture in slowly, giving the puppy time to swallow.
- Massage under the chin until all the mixture has gone (and to avoid having liquid spat all over you).

Never force the puppy's mouth wide open as it won't be able to swallow.

Puppy love — bonding time

For the first four months the puppy is getting to know its owners and its environment. When it is hungry it is fed; when it is frightened it is comforted; when it is lonely it is cuddled.

From seven weeks, puppies' brains are fully-developed and are like little computers waiting for information to be programmed in.

Between seven to 16 weeks they will learn things that will shape their characters as grown adult dogs. If they aren't taught by the owners in this time, they will find a way to learn other things on their own.

Between the ages of 12 and 16 weeks, puppies usually go through a stage similar to toddlers and their tantrums—the "terrible twos" and often become rebellious and defiant. When they reach 12 weeks old, they may even forget their house training, making a mess inside for no apparent reason. Happily, this is just a "phase" and lasts much less than with toddlers.

At three months, the puppy moves into a new behavioral stage and can become adventurous and willful. At this stage they need to learn control—the control of impulse. All of a sudden they aren't given food on demand when hungry and games aren't played when the puppy feels like playing. Frustration and bad behavior control must be guided carefully.

The puppy also has to learn about the rules of the household, who the boss is and what the rules are. Battles of will are fought without the puppy giving too much thought to the repercussions. The puppy's good sense is only just developing. It is also beginning to discover it can exercise quite a lot of control over humans. This leads to conflict!

Being puppies, they love being the center of attention. When you are on the phone the puppy may chew the telephone cord or pull off your slipper and cavort around the house

with it. When someone drops in for a chat it will jump up and down until someone takes notice and picks it up with cries of admiration.

A puppy will demand attention 24 hours a day—and more—and dominate the whole household. Most puppies have tunnel vision, which focuses only upon their own needs and happiness. When a puppy is playing and wants a particular thing to play with, it adopts a "smash and grab" approach. "Out of bounds" is something the owner must teach the puppy.

By the time it is 12 to 18 months old, the puppy is fast growing into a young dog. It exhibits more sense and observes the rules of the household. It thinks before it acts without inhibition.

Puppy behavior

Every owner wants the perfect puppy; happy-go-lucky and waggy tailed; one that loves the whole world, and is easy to train and is sociable.

Watch the puppy playing with other pups and you will see typical canine behavioral gestures:

Dominant: jumping on top of other puppies.

Submissive: rolling over on its back or onto its side.

Greeting: bottom sniffing.

Initiating play: head down, bottom up and a short bark.

Shy puppies are often more isolated, living and socializing with only the owner. They will hide under chairs and behind you when they meet people or other puppies and dogs. They need lots of socializing with both dogs and people. Take them out to parks and busy places to encourage the puppy to be confident. Under your supervision, let the puppy meet and be handled by both children and adults.

Bossy puppies are always going to be dominant animals and the most likely to show some aggression. The bossy puppy may get into noisy "fights" with other puppies and the owner will need to concentrate on controlling it. Keeping the puppy on a leash and restraining it when it shows aggressive behavior will begin the process of teaching it to control its behavior. If it is a large dog use a choker collar. You may need to seek help from professionals if the puppy is not responding to training.

Barking puppies may be just over-excited when socializing with people and other puppies, however barking is a potential problem. When it barks from the side-lines at children or other dogs, it needs calming. Praise and reward it when it stops barking. If the puppy barks excessively while playing, practice "time out." If the problem persists seek professional help.

Nasty habits

Adolescent male dogs can display inappropriate and unwanted approaches to human legs, as if they are about to mate, which leads to the hasty departure by most visitors who are unprepared for such bizarre, over-enthusiastic behavior. Small children can also be the innocent victims of "mounting" which can alarm parents.

It is a very common problem in young (both male and female) dogs but many people are so embarrassed by it they can't bring themselves to discuss it with their veterinarian. Don't be, it *is* a common problem and there are solutions.

It can usually be checked by diverting the puppy's attention. Try making a sudden, sharp noise such as "a clap" or drop something heavy, like a chain, on the floor. Say firmly: "Bah! No!" This also works with other misdirected sexual advances (to other dogs). Be very firm. Eventually, the clap, a rattle of the chain or a firm "Bah!" will stop the puppy's enthusiastic advances when Aunt Emily comes to call.

Once this aversion therapy is applied, the puppy's inappropriate sexual behavior should disappear. Seek veterinary advice about medication or neutering if its sex-drive (hyper-sexuality) is unabated.

Unless you intend to use the dog for breeding, castrating (at about nine months) is another option to put a stop to the male's stud gymnastics. Neutering will also help prevent the male dog's prostate problems in the future.

Repulsive habits

The sight of puppies (and grown dogs) eating their own droppings (called coprophagia) can be very shocking. (Some dogs also eat their vomit.) It is a hard habit to break.

It may be simply a depraved appetite caused by a mineral deficiency, in which case try giving it a mineral supplement and sprinkle yeast powder on its food. Alternatively, it could be a bored dog syndrome—a young active dog left alone all day with nothing to do or see. Pour chili or pepper sauce on any droppings you see as a very fiery dissuasion.

Bored dogs need at least a 20 minute walk or run every morning and night; and leave the puppy a nice bone to chew on, or even an old slipper or ball to play with.

If you catch your puppy in the act of eating its droppings, use the aversion therapy techniques discussed on the previous page: a sharp clap or the dropped chain followed with the firm "Bah! No!" Then bury the droppings, making sure you pour chili on them in case the puppy digs them up later. If you are not successful quickly seek veterinary advice.

Garden lovers

Puppies are easily bored and can get into all sorts of mischief when their owners are at work every day or even if just shut in the yard. A natural target then are garden plants.

Claude, a standard French poodle, once dug up 18 large prize camellias before the local dog shrink was called in. Unfortunately his owner had no success with the analyst's prescription for taking control of the dog, but she and Claude moved to the mountains (and a new yard without camellias) where she retired. That solved the digging-up-the-garden-beds problem, because the dog then stayed indoors (sleeping on the bed) except for long walks which he hadn't enjoyed while his owner had worked in the city.

Other stronger-minded (or plant-proud) owners eventually get the hang of going into the yard with the dog and being very firm ("No!") when it even begins scratching the ground. Exercise and toys to chew will most likely help the problem—or some owners even resort to getting a second dog for company.

Ankle biters

Most people will offer a tiny puppy their finger to bite or chew but as its teeth get sharper and stronger, it is not a sensation many of us continue to enjoy. As the puppy plays, it will jump up and grab hold of a hand or arm with its very sharp teeth or bite the nearest ankle.

The command "No!" and "Ouch!" should be said with monotonous regularity every time the puppy attempts to bite even in play. If the puppy keeps biting, stop the game, ignoring the puppy and walk out of the room. Do not hit the puppy or push it out of the way; it interprets this as a game and will keep on biting. If all else fails enforce "time out" until the puppy has calmed down.

Remind family and visitors not to encourage hand biting. Rough house play with a small puppy may result in a snappy grown dog later on, so children must be stopped from doing this.

If the small puppy growls at you coming near when it is eating, during the next meal hold the dish with your hands until it has finished eating. If the puppy growls aggressively when the owner gives it a bone, take the bone away to enforce just who is "boss dog." The owner should never be nervous of small puppy aggression; this is the time to teach and control it with firmness and kindness.

A grown dog who snaps and bites at people should wear a muzzle and an identifying collar with a strong leash. Dogs can be destroyed or declared dangerous for biting a person or another animal.

Mailman ambush

The daily arrival of the mailman is usually announced by distant barking which rises

to an approaching crescendo as the resident dogs rush towards mail boxes. Dogs not confined by fences lunge at the mailman's legs with fierce shouting as the mailman breaks free.

This sort of puppy delinquency must be nipped firmly in the bud. If your puppy is showing signs of anti-mailman tendencies, walk the dog using a choke chain when you expect the mailman and, when it barks or lunges at him, gently jerk the chain while firmly growling "No!"

If the mailman is still speaking to you, let him know the puppy's name and ask him to call it out loudly every time he approaches until it recognizes him as a friend.

Living with the enemy—cats

Co-existing with cats worries owners when they bring home a new puppy. Old street-wise cats will usually set the ground rules when the puppy pounces exuberantly around them, barking excitedly, by settling the argument with some hissing and a quick paw swipe if the puppy gets too close.

The owner must set some ground rules as well, speaking very firmly to the puppy if it tries to chase the cat. Usually they sort themselves out, like children, after their initial introduction and spats. One of the first lessons the puppy must learn and obey is "No!" when it looks as if it is even thinking about chasing cats.

When a new kitten is introduced to a young puppy, the kitten will soon take control. If possible choose a fearless kitten who will stand its ground and not be frightened when you let in the puppy.

Car chasing

This is one of the most dangerous activities for puppies who may imagine they are back in the wild herding animals or just enjoying the thrill of the chase. It results in many puppies being killed or badly injured, and can be the cause of fatal road accidents. It is hard to break the instinct—teaching the puppy to obey "No!" and "Stay!" are the best solutions. However, if the habit can't be broken keep the puppy confined on a leash or, when it is older, a choker.

A puppy, or even a grown dog, should never be allowed on the street without a leash—it is simply too dangerous.

Jumping on people

Puppies will leap on the owner full of enthusiasm and love when they come home. At first this is encouraged but when the growing puppy does the same to visitors, they may not be quite so delighted. The puppy is told to get down immediately and is then confused because the owner is not being consistent. As the puppy grows heavier, the owner may not enjoy its hard head hitting them on the nose, muddy paw prints on their clothing, torn and laddered stockings or a sloppy "kiss" during the ecstatic canine welcome.

Practice putting a knee lightly forward into the puppy's chest as it goes to jump up, saying, "No! Down!" Ignore it until the puppy responds and stops trying to leap up. The owner should then lean down and make a big fuss of the puppy at its level.

Idle puppies

Some puppies love stealing things — baby's soft toys, socks, shoes, stockings and garments from the laundry basket. They dig holes in the yard, tear out plants and bark too much—these are all signs of boredom, but habits nevertheless that need to be avoided. If you catch the puppy in one of these acts of treachery try using the aversion therapy—the clap or chain and the command, "Bah! No!"—until the puppy gets your message.

Don't punish the puppy after it has committed the crime as it does not understand punishment in retrospect, and you will only end up with a very confused and frightened puppy as well as torn and chewed belongings.

Like little children it is wiser to remove temptations like shoes and clothing that have been left lying around on the floor. Puppies *love* to chew so provide them with more appropriate toys than your belongings—puppy chews, rubber bones, balls and other indestructible toys.

Hole digging

Some puppies love digging holes in gardens or lawns. Dogs instinctively bury caches of bones to scavenge later, and if they've recently had a large meal they will bury food they don't want to eat. Give the puppy chewing substitutes to gnaw instead of bones. Leave it with suitable toys providing hours of entertainment and change them often to keep the puppy interested and away from plants and lawn. In hot weather, some dogs will dig sleeping holes in the cool, damp earth around shrubs and under trees. Fill the dug holes with stones, then cover with soil, to discourage more digging in that spot. A good kennel provided from puppyhood in a sheltered section of the yard should offer shade and refuge from the hot summer sun. It may be best to fence off gardens with stakes and wire mesh, and use plastic tree guards to save plants and shrubs until the puppy learns some yard manners.

Barking

Puppies bark—and bark and bark. It is a normal phenomenon, yet neighbors still complain. Puppies bark as a greeting, or in the anticipated joy of a walk, or as a loud warning that a stranger (the mailman, delivery men or a visitor) is invading their territory, or that they can see another dog on the sidewalk, or a cat sunning itself on a rooftop. It may be barking for attention, or simply for water, or to get out of the sun or cold wind—dogs left in the yard all day must have fresh water and shelter from sun and rain.

Some breeds are predisposed to bark more than others, but training to modify their barking is possible. Dogs usually bark when they are lonely or bored. Again, exercise the puppy for 20 minutes each morning and evening. Leave it in a confined area with its water (in a solid dish that can't be knocked over), food and toys. A radio left playing quietly on a talk station will also be company in these early days.

It is also good canine psychology to pat the puppy, telling it to "stay" before you leave. If it starts barking, use the previously described aversion therapy. Repeat until the barking stops. And don't forget to lavishly praise the puppy when it quiets down.

Some pups may be barking out of fear or they may be barking to relieve the tension of solitary confinement all day in a backyard. A "dog door," giving the puppy access to even a back room of the house may make the puppy settle down. Also look for advertisements (local newspapers, pet stores and vet clinics) for dog-sitters or dog walkers available in the area who may exercise the puppy during the day. The puppy may bark less after the extra exercise.

If the puppy still barks all day despite your efforts, it may need specialist help from your veterinary clinic or one of the many animal behaviorist services who receive thousands of calls every month about barking from worried dog owners.

These services will arrange home visits to find the cause of the dog's behavior and suggestions for a cure. Much depends on the owner's commitment to working with the puppy.

The only other alternatives are the controversial electronic bark inhibitor collar which emits a high-pitched ultrasonic "zing" when stimulated by the laryngeal movements of the dog, and "de-barking" or the legalized surgical alteration by a veterinarian of the pitch of a dog's bark. There is still a bark but the vocal chords will be much softer or huskier.

New age puppies

The underlying causes of a puppy's physical and emotional problems may be revealed by alternative practices. The healing art of Reiki, the literal laying on of hands to bring prana or chi (life force energy) to areas of the body or soul is regularly used by alternative veterinary clinics. Reiki sessions usually last around 40 minutes to find and cure the underlying causes of an animal's physical problems. It works on the deepest level—mere physical symptoms of anxiety or aggression are usually manifestations of unhappiness or lifestyle.

Increasingly used are homeopathic and Bach flower remedies (herbal drops used for improving moods without adversely affecting the physical condition) for disturbed and stressed pets.

Stress is mostly caused just by puppies being left alone too long, not getting enough attention and exercise. Dogs often become depressed when children grow up and leave the family home or one of the family dies.

Acupuncture works on behavioral and emotional problems too, particularly grief and bereavement.

If puppies chase their tails or bark at shadows, it is a coping mechanism for dealing with something wrong in its lifestyle. Changes must be made, including counselling the owner.

The Doggie Diner

The Doggie Diner

Healthy, easy to prepare,
homemade food for
your dog

Marie Toshack

SMITHMARK

With thanks to all the good friends who delved into their favorite homemade recipe collections, particularly Pat Fleet, Kath Wilson, Helen Rook and their families of animals.

Sincere thanks for the generous and freely given time and expert help from Dr. Arthur Poynting, of the Gloucester Veterinary Hospital, and the staff of the Gladesville Animal Hospital, Sydney, in particular Dr. Max Zuber and Dr. Pam Short.

The publishers would like to thank Scott McGregor and Wendy Gray and their dog "Patsy," Lucian Francis and minature Poodle "Toshka," Lola Pinder and Weimaraner "Dusty," Francis and Tibetan terrier "Buffy," Margaret Cloonan and Kerry Blue "Rose," Lois and Cec Way and Pug "Patrin Abit Ofa Newsince," Sandra Francis and Dalmation "Tasha," Isabella Manfredi and minature Fox terrier "Missy," Cocker spaniel "Ziggy," and King Charles spaniel "Saba." Also thanks to the Royal New South Wales Canine Council Ltd, Seaforth Veterinary Hospital, Oliver Strewe and Ernie Kaltenbach.

Contents

BEFORE buying a dog, think about your budget. If you are drawn to the big, long-haired aristocratic breeds, that look magnificent on the screen and in the showring, remember that they do grow up with enormous appetites, and need grooming and walking every day.

Think of house pet potential: big dogs, the size of German shepherds and Great Danes, don't adjust well to living in small apartments. Long-haired breeds, like the Samoyeds or Maltese, feel the heat. Tiny chihuahuas need extra heating in winter. Smaller breeds, which don't shed hair, may be better indoors. Some little dogs are yappy, very yappy. Big dogs will need at least an hour's workout every day — and eat more than little dogs, which can be very fussy and finicky when it comes to food. Some dogs can be anorexic; others eat everything in sight. Backyard and guard dogs eat a lot more. Old and sick dogs need special and expensive diets.

Look at the enormous range of supermarket pet foods, and the cost. There is a huge difference in what dogs eat, from the tiny toy terriers to the big breeds, and this makes a big difference to their running costs, plus grooming and other built-in extras like immunization and preventative medication.

Select-a-dog

Pug

Tend towards gluttony, but are pleasant pets. Can have snoring, snorting and skin problems, and those table manners need watching, but if they stick to their diets-for-size they won't break the budget.

Cavalier King Charles spaniel

These pretty dogs are always in dog food commercials and on TV pet shows. Will eat everything in sight (including the cat food), but need watching, as they can become fussy eaters. They have loving natures and they need lots of attention, walks and games.

Australian terrier

Wiry little watchdogs and excellent pets, that seem to be bred for a life indoors but surprisingly adapt well to the countryside; like poodles, they have been known to take to farm work with a passion. Fearless, they will tackle snakes or burglars, or fly into ferocious dog fights, but look for them under the bed in a thunderstorm. They are not fussy eaters, and would kill for a taste of the cat's milk.

Chihuahua Tiny Mexican dogs—small, smart, loyal and their bark makes them good guard dogs. Greedy (begs at table) and fussy. It's best to give them several small meals a day. Cheap to feed for size (smallest dog in the world).

Basset hound Big dogs with big appetites. They need a varied diet, meat and vegetables with lots of calcium for that big frame. Bred for hunting but happy to spend the day just lying around the house or backyard.

Beagle Sturdy, with a tendency to be portly. Watch their weight, as they'll eat anything. Pick a diet that includes lots of vegetables and rice mixed with either canned or cooked protein. No eating between meals at home, next door or along the street.

Dalmatian In fashion again since the *101 Dalmatians* movie. Tend to be a bit greedy. A good diet is required for these big, powerful dogs.

Deerhound Can you afford to feed giants?

Great Dane Enormous appetites—a big bank account and a well-stocked freezer is required. Eats 3 lb /1.5 kg daily. Make it a varied diet, lots of calcium and phosphorus for those huge frames.

Newfoundland St. Bernard, Pyrenean mountain dog. You'll need your own butcher store for these minority breeds, but they'll eat anything served up to them. And they are gentle with children. Don't forget the grooming costs.

Hungarian Puli Amazing ragtag dreadlock coat on four legs. Weighs up to 30 lb/15 kg. Include in diet vegetables, chicken, beef and dried food.

Poodle One of the world's favorite house dogs, not only because their double coats don't shed on carpets or furniture, but they are fairly safe with asthmatics. Grooming is a lifelong expense. Affectionate, playful natures, and love company. Not just pretty faces, some are excellent working dogs in the country. Fussy eaters if indulged.

Jack Russell terrier Very fashionable, have been elevated from ratters to society accessories. Small eaters that are very cheap to keep.

Scottish terrier Scotties will eat any canned food, fresh or cooked meat

and dried food, and must watch the kilos. They have a tendancy to put on weight if they do not get enough exercise. There are grooming costs too.

Fox terrier (foxy) Excitable, excellent watchdogs and rat-catchers. Small eaters.

Cocker spaniel This happy-go-lucky breed must sign up for Weight Watchers; prone to gormandizing and piling on the weight.

Labrador retriever

Labradors need to keep fit or they'll get fat. They make placid, easygoing pets and are ideal guide-dogs. Happy to eat canned and dry dog food and any left-overs; won't break the budget.

Mutt The "no-names" from lost dog's homes make good, loving family pets. They are from interesting backgrounds but are happy to be part of the family. Depending on their eventual size (always look at a puppy's paws; big feet means big dog), costs can range from only a little to a great deal!

Maltese Sweet, devoted balls of white fur that are a very popular fashion accessory (grooming or clipping is required in hot summer weather), but they are tough and cheap to feed.

Rottweiler Big and muscular with an uncertain temperament, Rottweilers are strong dogs, nearly the same size as the Rhodesian ridgebacks, 76 lbs/38 kg of muscle. Neither dog has a special diet — would you refuse them a feed, though?

Staffordshire terrier

These friendly little dogs are often confused with the savage attacks by crossbreeds and the more aggressive pit bulls. Staffies, the smiling little brindle dogs with the bow legs, are very affectionate. Loyal but jealous — the reason for those wide, strong collars is to drag them apart from other dogs who come near their owner. Fearless. A friend used to tell the story of a hapless burglar held down by the legs of two determined Staffies all Sunday afternoon until the owners returned. Not fussy eaters.

Boxer Headstrong and bouncy. Never really grow up. Need to burn off boundless energy chasing cats up trees. They eat well because they are such a big, strong breed.

Doberman Low-maintenance, often placid "attack" dogs. Long, lean, fine boned dogs – it's an urban myth that one ate

its owner. Should keep their food bowls always filled—but don't overfeed them. Give sensible meals of meat (raw or cooked) and kibble. Obedience classes essential.

Greyhound

Needs a minimum of 45 minutes exercise a day, plus racing and just chasing things—eats plenty of fresh meat and kibble, which might cost a lot. Muzzling is an extra cost.

Australian cattle dog

"True blue" kelpies, blue heelers and black and white collies—these dogs work hard and live hard. Tied up to kennels made out of old drums, far from the farmhouse, they have lean and hungry figures, and are on their feet all day, chasing after cattle, horses or sheep. As suburban pets, they are cheap to feed, will eat any food—even the sheets and towels on the washing line, if bored. Doubling as guard dogs in tiny backyards puts on the weight; their coats lose their luster and an evening stroll is not enough for them to keep their edge.

Schnauzer

A favorite breed that comes in three sizes with appetites to match. Grooming costs (regular stripping and clipping) are involved, but schnauzers don't shed all over the furniture. Whiskery face, bushy eyebrows and moustache, with big square body, give the schnauzer a delightful "old man" appearance.

Weimaraner

Tawny yellow eyes and driftwood-colored coats. The "grey ghosts" are not deep thinkers, but stay young at heart. They love to run about a lot in parks.

Saluki

Not inexpensive to keep, with elegantly slim, long legs and weighing quite a bit. They are bred for hunting and need at least an hour's walk a day. Grooming is an extra cost.

Irish wolfhound

This giant breed is the tallest dog in the world, which rules it out for most apartments, even most homes. Too placid for guard duties, but Wolfie's size is enough to frighten off any muggers on daily walks. A big eater that requires plenty of exercise.

Skye terrier

"In a quiet corner... Bobby had the leavings of a herring or haddie, for a rough little Skye will eat anything from smoked fish to moor-fowl eggs, and he had the titbit of a fathing bone to worry at his leisure." (Eleanor Atkinson, *Greyfriars Bobby*, Puffin Books, first published 1940). These tough little dogs look like frantic floppy mops on legs. Skye-born

Bobby was a barker and nipper of shins ("in pure exuberance of spirits") then asking questions later—something the Skyes are noted for. Close-set eyes, hidden by long floppy hair falling over the head. Eats very little (less if fathing bones and moor-fowl eggs are still available).

Afghan

Old English sheepdog, Briard. Fallen comrades of fickle fashion fads for dogs, Afghans took hours of grooming for that Farrah Fawcett look. Tall, rather nervy dogs who can race with the wind, long fur streaming, Afghans are still around and it's a sad sight to see those flowing "trousers" clipped. Also passé are the lovable, goofy-looking Old English sheepdogs (the original shaggy dogs of the 1970s), who need daily blowdries or savage chopping. The scruffy, long-haired Briards could be the Next Big Thing of grunge among the long-haired bigger breeds because, frankly, grooming is wasted. They aren't finicky and will scoff down any food.

Shar Pei

Darlings of the high fashion magazines, draped with jewels over their incredibly wrinkled, crinkled folds of skin. Next Big Thing or just the world's wrinkliest dogs? Chinese tomb guard dogs that look like fat Buddhas, Shar Peis are a relatively new and expensive breed. They could have earning potential modelling?

Bichon frisé

About the size of the Maltese, and the Bouvier des Flandres, another attractive newcomer, these are dogs to watch.

Feeding your dog

More than any other aspect of the dog's development, proper feeding requires an educated and responsible owner. A dog is a pretty robust character that will protect your house, bark at strangers, walk or sit quietly with you and eagerly fetch whatever you throw—but it still counts on you to take care of its needs.

Dogs are principally carnivores, or meat-eaters. But vegetables, fruit and berries are natural supplements to their diets. A pure meat diet is deficient in many things. Meat should not exceed 20–25 percent of the dog's total diet.

Essential components of a dog's diet are protein—meat, eggs, cheese, milk and vitamins, minerals and carbohydrates—vegetables, pasta and cereals. Protein is well digested

by the dog and is the basic building block for animal tissue. Vitamins, minerals and carbohydrates are also essential components to your dog's diet.

The new puppy

As soon as the weaned pup comes home, it will need to be fed four times a day. Always find out from the breeder what the puppy has been fed, as a sudden change in a dog's diet may cause bowel upsets.

Like babies, puppies (who shouldn't leave their mothers until they are eight or nine weeks old) need lots of sleep during the first few weeks. On its first nights alone in the new home, a hot water bottle wrapped in a towel and a ticking clock near its bed will act as substitutes for the warmth and heart-beats of its mother and siblings.

Teach the puppy good feeding habits from the start, placing the food bowl on a newspaper on the kitchen or laundry-room floor. Allow a reasonable time to eat, then pick up the bowl and don't offer any more food until next meal time.

Always have fresh, clean drinking water handy and a newspaper or shallow litter tray on the floor, for the start of house-training. (Not all puppies come house-trained, as some new owners fondly imagine.)

The puppy's diet should be as the breeder has recommended, or based on a good commercial food, labeled "balanced" or "complete." Remember, the most expensive foods need not be the best; however, the very cheapest brands are not necessarily "balanced." You can use baby cereal or oatmeal porridge or special puppy cereals soaked in milk. Avoid using a single brand or product, as the puppy may become too fussy and refuse to eat anything else.

Two months old to twelve weeks old

Morning: 5 or 6 tablespoons of cow's milk at room temperature. If cow's milk is too strong, try a simple very digestible mix of half evaporated milk and half water, mixed with 3 to 5 tablespoons of puppy meal or baby cereal to a creamy consistency.

Noon: 1 to 2 heaped tablespoons of raw ground beef (at room temperature) with a liquid or powdered vitamin supplement. In addition, half a teaspoon of cod-liver oil and a sprinkling of bonemeal can be given. Cooked mashed vegetables can be added.

Afternoon: Same as the morning meal — always at room temperature.

Evening: As for noon meal, plus milk.

Bedtime: More milk.

Three months old

Morning: About 3/4 cup milk, mixed with 5 or 6 tablespoons of puppy meal or baby

cereal to a creamy consistency.
Noon: 3 to 4 heaped tablespoons ground meat, plus the vitamin supplement, and cod-liver oil.
Afternoon: Same as noon meal.
Evening: Same as morning meal.

Four and five months old

Morning: 1 1/2 cups milk mixed with 1 cup of good dog meal or cereal mixed to a porridge-like consistency.
Noon: Depending on the size of the dog serve chopped or ground beef with 1/2 teaspoon cod-liver oil and a sprinkling of bonemeal plus vitamin supplement.
Late afternoon: Repeat noon meal.
Evening: Repeat morning meal. Warm milk or soupy oatmeal given last thing before bed will continue to settle the puppy down.

At six months, drop the lunchtime meal. At nine months, serve a token breakfast and give the main meal in late afternoon or evening (toy and small dogs may require smaller meals during the day to keep their blood sugar levels up.)

Adult dogs

Adult dogs will thrive on all diet types from basic canned food, complete dried food and left-overs to gourmet homemade dishes. Occasional treats won't hurt. Read the labels to make sure the commercial food contains protein (meat, fish, eggs, cheese, milk), carbohydrate (biscuit, kibble, rice, pasta), vegetables (carrots, potatoes, pumpkin, celery, parsley, tomatoes, spinach, onions, garlic) and fat.

The dinner box

Meat is the easiest digested and most popular food with dogs. Some meats, such as pork and liver, are best served to your dog cooked because of the risk of parasites.

Eggs are a good source of protein but are best served cooked because raw egg white can interfere with your dog's vitamin metabolism. Raw egg yolk on its own is fine.

Cheese is another good source of protein although too much may give your dog diarrhea and it can also contribute to overweight problems. It is also an excellent source of calcium which is necessary for strong bones.

Milk is a good source of calcium but some dogs may have difficulty digesting milk because of the lactose it contains.

Cereals and pasta are a good source of carbohydrates which is a ready energy source for your dog.

Vegetables are good for your dog because they provide vitamins and minerals. They can be cooked to make them more digestible

but finely grated is fine too. Potatoes are not easily digested and should be cooked because they can sometimes cause wind. Peas and beans are excellent as is raw grated zucchini. Vegetables are best mixed in with other foods to make them more palatable rather than served alone.

Fat also has its place in your dog's diet. A small amount of fat should be left on any meat that is served. Dogs digest fat well and it helps keep their coats lustrous. Too much fat however can have the same effect on your dog as it would on humans. It can lead to disease, obesity and poor health.

Fish is a good food for dogs but should be cooked (and boneless) as it has an enzyme that can destroy vital vitamins if it is eaten uncooked. It is packed with protein, minerals and some fats. Some dogs may not like fish no matter how it is prepared.

Honey is a great source of vitamins and minerals and is recommended by herbalists for dogs.

Nuts and edible seeds are all excellent additions to the diet.

Bones can cause problems such as constipation, or obstruction or perforation of the digestive tract. Only give raw bones that are broad and marrow-filled so that they do not splinter. An exception to this are raw chicken wings which will not cause any harm to your dog. Include raw bones (it's an old wives' tale that bones make dogs savage) in your dog's diet. Butchers will saw up large marrow bones, which will keep the dog's teeth in good order. Some breeders are not happy to feed their dogs bones, however most veterinarians agree that raw bones are very good for dogs. Cooked bones should never be given to your dog.

Fruit is a surprisingly natural addition to your dog's diet. In the wild, dogs supplement their diet with wild berries and fruits. Small quantities of fruit occasionally is beneficial. Dogs do not need vitamin C because they make their own internally.

Doggie diets

Dog foods tailored for special purposes—slimming, geriatric care, allergies, chronic liver, kidney and heart diseases—are available from vets in convenient dried and canned ranges. But homemade recipes are also available.

Weight control

Fat dogs, like fat people, are liable to die young. Overweight dogs can develop arthritis, degenerative back disease, hip dysplasia, gallstones, liver cirrhosis, heart and lung diseases, diabetes and hypertension. Owners (often overweight and middle-aged

Guide to normal weights of common breeds

Breed	Dog pounds	Dog kilos	Bitch pounds	Bitch kilos
Afgan hound	59-70	27-32	51-66	23-30
Airedale terrier	44-51	20-23	44-51	20-23
Kelpie	45-55	20-25	40-59	18-27
Silky terrier	8-19	3-5	8-19	3-5
Basenji	24	11	22	10
Basset hound	40-59	18-27	35-50	16-23
Beagle	29-35	13-16	24-29	11-13
Border collie	42-53	19-24	40-48	18-22
Boxer	66	30	62	28
British bulldog	55	25	51	23
Bull terrier	40-51	18-23	40-50	18-23
Staffordshire terrier	29-37	13-17	24-26	11-13
King Charles spaniel	10-18	4-8	10-12	4-8
Chihuahua	2-7	1-3	2-7	1-3
Collie	45-65	20-30	40-50	18-25
Dachshund long hair	18	8	18	8
Dachshund smooth hair	24	11	22	10
Dachshund wire hair	20-22	9-10	18-22	8-9
Dalmation	59	27	55	25
Dobermann	75-90	34-41	65-79	29-36
Fox terrier	15-18	7-8	15-18	7-8
German shepherd	75-85	34-39	59-70	27-32

Breed	Dog pounds	Dog kilos	Bitch pounds	Bitch kilos
German short-hair pointer	55-70	25-32	44-59	20-27
Great Dane	120	54	100	45
Greyhound	66-70	30-32	59-66	27-30
Labrador	59	27	55	25
Maltese	4-9	2-4	4-9	2-4
Newfoundland	140-150	63-68	100-120	50-55
Old English sheepdog	59-90	27-41	51-59	23-27
Pekingese	8	3	8-12	3-6
Pomeranian	4	2	4-5	2-3
Poodle standard	64-74	29-34	65-74	29-34
Poodle miniature	11-15	5-7	11-15	5-7
Poodle toy	8-12	3-6	8-12	3-6
Golden retriever	66-70	30-32	55-59	25-27
Rottweiler	100-120	45-55	79-90	36-41
Samoyed	45-55	20-25	35-45	16-21
English setter	59-66	27-30	55-62	25-28
Irish setter	59-66	27-30	55-59	25-27
Cocker spaniel	24-29	11-13	24-29	11-13
American cocker spaniel	24-29	11-13	24-29	11-13
Springer spaniel	51	23	51	23
Welsh corgi	22-26	10-12	20-24	9-11
Whippet	22-29	10-13	18-24	8-11

themselves) never believe that their dog is too fat, but surveys show that up to 40 percent of dogs are overweight. Once too fat, the dogs become lethargic, do less exercise and become fatter.

After a careful examination by a vet, weigh the dog every week (stand on the bathroom scales alone, then carrying the dog, and the difference equals the dog's weight), measure the dog's food and once the target weight is reached keep the dog on a maintenance diet. Begin an exercise program, starting off with a thirty-minute brisk walk.

Neighbors who can't resist those melting, begging eyes, must be reminded that tidbits are coffin nails. No more table scraps, no cookies, no chocolates, keep the lid tight on the garbage can, take more walks (good for the owners too) and take a new approach to the dog's food plan. From veterinarians there are commercially prepared low-fat, high-fiber and high-nutrient diets available for fat dogs.

Calories must be restricted to 60 percent of the maintenance diet for their ideal weight, and divide their daily allowance into two or three feedings, with fresh water always available. Change "snacks" to low-calorie squares of bread or a whole carrot to fool the dog into believing it's eating something substantial instead of a Jenny Craig-style treat.

Lean and mean low-fat reducing diet

4 oz/125g lean ground or minced beef
3 oz/75g cottage cheese (low fat, 90% water and high quality protein)
2 cups carrots, canned or cooked, grated
2 cups green beans, cooked, chopped
1 1/2 teaspoons dicalcium phosphate

Cook the beef in a hot pan. Drain off any fat and cool. Add the rest of the ingredients and mix into the meat. Large bones, well trimmed, or even a long carrot, will keep the dog busy chewing.

A Basic Diet

A 16–22 lb/8–11 kg dog should have the following elements in its diet. Amounts for a basic and a weight reduction diet are shown.

	Basic	Reduction
ground meat	1/3 cup (med fat)	1/3 cup (lean)
rice (raw)	2/3 cup	1/3 (or less)
bran (dry)	2/3 cup	1/3 (or less)
liver	3 teaspoons	1 teaspoon
bonemeal	3 teaspoons	3 teaspoons
corn oil	1 teaspoon	1 teaspoon
iodized salt	1/2 teaspoon	1/2 teaspoon
water	2 cups	2 cups

Boil rice until cooked. Add bran to make a gruel, which firms as it cools. (More bran and less rice is better for weight reduction, but dogs don't find the bran very palatable. Experiment with different grains, oats, rice and bran). Add meat and liver and other ingredients, simmer for 10 minutes, then

cool. Can be stored in a refrigerator for a few days, or frozen.

Low-fat high-fiber canine diet

3 oz/75g rice
2/3 cup bran
3 oz/75g very lean meat, minced or ground
Cook the rice in water and add the bran. Stir in the meat, adding more water.

Vet's advice: Prevention of obesity requires care at every step of the dog's life. It's the eye of the owner which fattens the puppy, the young, the middle-aged and the old dog. It is often the owner who needs re-training, to change the dog's feeding habits. Losing the weight is relatively easy, but avoiding a relapse is notoriously hard, because it is a lifetime habit.

Food allergies

Like a person, a dog can develop a bowel upset from food allergies. Or its head can swell up like a football, with swollen eyes and puffy lips. Antihistamine injections will reduce the swelling.

If you go to an allergy clinic, they'll put you on an elimination diet first. It's the same with dogs. Most dried and canned commercial foods (for people and dogs) contain preservatives and artificial colorings as well as grains, and are the first to go from the diet. White meats, brown rice, potatoes and sunflower or safflower vegetable oils are a safe start for an allergy-free, home-cooked diet.

Dogs with skin conditions often benefit from an allergy diet.

Hypo-allergenic diet (dogs and cats)

4 oz/125g lamb (rabbit, venison, chicken, turkey or fish may be substituted), steamed, simmered or ground raw
1 cup cooked brown rice
1 teaspoon vegetable oil
1 1/2 teaspoons calcium phosphate powder
Combine all the ingredients and mix well.

Vet's advice: Try something the dog does not usually eat, and avoid beef, dairy foods (including milk), sugary foods and wheat products. Gluten—found in wheat, oats, barley and rye—is not contained in rice or maize. Ailing dogs should respond to the meatier ratio of one part rice to two parts meat. A prescription diet is also available from vets for dogs with suspected food allergies.

Geriatric diets

Depending on the breed of the dog, it is considered "geriatric" after 5–7 years (a sobering thought for even thirty-something owners.) This introduces whole new canine medical conditions: some dogs will be overweight, others too thin (even anorexic), others will be chronic invalids, while others

will be as energetic and frisky as younger pups.

Older dogs need about 40 percent less calories than younger dogs, but they still require the correct nutritional balance. Try to avoid salt. Add boiled rice and pasta to the dog's diet and avoid starchy, rich, sugary food — even as treats.

Seniors stew

4 oz/125g meat (retain any fat), minced and lightly simmered
1 hard-boiled egg, chopped or mashed
2 cups cooked brown rice (no salt)
2 slices white bread, crumbled
1 teaspoon calcium carbonate

Mix all together. Add warm water until the mixture has a good consistency for the dog to eat.

Stress diet

1/3 cup dry rice
1 cup fatty beef
4 cups water
1 tablespoon corn oil
2 teaspoons bonemeal
1 teaspoon iodized salt
1 ice cube of liver
(Cut liver into small pieces, pack into ice cube trays and freeze until needed.)

Bring the water to a boil with the oil, bonemeal and salt. Add the rice and simmer for 10 minutes. Add the chopped meat and the liver; simmer for 10 minutes more. Don't overcook. This mixture can be cooked in larger batches and frozen for convenience.

Vet's advice: Provide the stressed dog with a sound diet of at least 30% protein. Train the dog to handle stressful situations and avoid stress by giving tender loving care.

Kidney and bladder stones

Dogs recovering from bladder stones should avoid dried food, which tends to concentrate the urine, and they should have plenty of fresh water.

Low-sodium diet

4 oz/125g good lean ground beef (poultry, or non-oily fish)
2 cups cooked brown rice (no salt)
2 teaspoons dicalcium phosphate

Braise the meat, retaining the fat. Add the rest of the ingredients and mix.

Vet's warning: Dogs on low-salt diets (usually for heart and kidney failure conditions) should never be fed processed foods – half a sausage would send the diet out the window. (Basically, follow the same diet rules for people.)

Female urinary-problems diet

Dogs, specially elderly spade bitches, can suffer from bladder infections (cystitis)

which change the pH balance in the urine. Besides causing pain like razor blades, the urine leaves round dead patches in the lawn (or bleaches the carpet). Bladder stones produce similar symptoms to cystitis. Besides collecting a sample (a well-washed, sterilized and discreetly-placed plastic dust pan or dish is the shot) for the vet to prescribe treatment, you can avoid recurrences with careful attention to the dog's diet – this should also clean up the lawn, if not the carpet.

Cut the meat (protein) content back to less than 40%, use 40% vegetables—beans, carrots, pumpkin, squash and especially parsley—and 20% rice or pasta. Give plenty of fresh drinking water.

Restricted protein/phosphorus diet

4 oz/125g ground beef (don't use lean meat)
1 large egg
2 cups cooked rice (no salt)
3 slices white bread, crumbled
1 teaspoon calcium carbonate powder

Braise the meat in a pan, reserving the fat. While hot, mix well with all the remaining ingredients. If too dry, add some water—not milk.

Low protein stew

1 lb/500g chicken or fish, minced
2 cans tomatoes, chopped
6 big potatoes, chopped
2 large onions, chopped
1 cup wholemeal macaroni
1 lb/500g dry rice
2 cups water
2 cups juice from cooking beans and carrots (or from canned vegetables, beans or carrots)

Cook all ingredients together in a large casserole, in a medium oven for about 1 1/2 hours. This makes a large stew.

Homemade

Homemade diets are preferred for a variety of reasons. Some owners believe that fresh ingredients, including vegetables and rice are purer and safer. Some owners worry about the preservatives in store-bought pet foods and the health of their dogs, and still others want to give their dogs a varied diet.

Vegetarians must take care not to impose their own food preferences on their pets. It is very difficult to develop a balanced diet for dogs (and impossible for cats) that is free of products from animal sources.

Home-baked doggie treats

Not all dog food comes in sacks from the supermarket. You can bake your own, free of food dyes and preservatives.

INGREDIENTS

2 meat stock cubes
6 cups milk (or water)
4 lb/2 kg wholewheat flour
5 oz/165g oatmeal
3 1/2 tablespoons oil
vitamin powder

METHOD

Dissolve the stock cubes in the milk or water. Mix together the flour, oatmeal and oil. Add the flavored milk or water. Add the vitamin powder and work into a stiff consistency. Roll into small sausage shapes, then bake on a greased tray in a slow oven until brown and crisp. These cookies could be flavored with extra chicken extract or liver juice. The dried food is excellent chewing for teeth and gums (to prevent tartar) and the absence of food dyes and preservatives is better for the dog.

Blue Jean's meatloaf with chicken

INGREDIENTS

1 lb/500g ground steak
(include some fat; dogs need fat)
4 chicken sausages
1 carrot, grated
2 zucchini, grated
1 onion, grated
2 cloves garlic, chopped finely
3 eggs
$^1/_2$ cup wholewheat breadcrumbs

Topping:
extra breadcrumbs
$^1/_2$ cup of cheese (optional)

METHOD

Mix all the ingredients together except the chicken sausages and the topping. Add a little milk if it's not the right consistency—it shouldn't be too sloppy, as the vegetables will give the loaf extra moisture as it cooks. Put half the mixture into a large greased loaf pan, then add the sausages lengthwise along the pan, then put in the rest of the mixture. Press down to make an even surface and sprinkle with the topping. Bake in a moderate oven until the sides of the meat loaf leave the pan. Cool and cut into servings. The remainder can be stored in the refrigerator or freezer.

Fegato with gravy

INGREDIENTS

2 lb/1 kg beef liver
2 slices ham, pork or bacon
2 cups wholemeal breadcrumbs
3 cloves garlic, peeled and sliced
2 eggs, slightly beaten
2 tablespoons wholewheat flour
oil
1 $^{1}/_{2}$ cups water
$^{1}/_{2}$ cup well-cooked (soft) rice, optional

METHOD

Place the liver in bowl and cover it with boiling water. Leave it to stand for 10 minutes, then drain. In a food processor, mix the liver with the slices of ham, add crumbs, sliced garlic and eggs and mix thoroughly. Press into a loaf tin and bake in a moderate oven for about an hour until the top has browned. Remove the loaf from the oven and remove from the pan. Heat the oil in a pan and stir in 2 tablespoons of wholemeal flour to make a paste. Then slowly pour in the cold water and stir over a low heat for about 5 minutes until the gravy thickens.

Cooked rice can be added to the gravy. Pour the gravy over slices of the liver loaf. The remainder of the loaf and gravy can be stored in the fridge or freezer.

Major's liver

(for small dogs)

INGREDIENTS

2 lb/1 kg liver
1 onion, peeled and chopped
1 cloves garlic, peeled and sliced
vegetable oil
$^{1}/_{2}$ cup rice
1 tablespoon parsley, finely chopped

METHOD

Slice the liver into short thin strips. Boil the rice until soft. Stew the chopped onion and sliced garlic with the oil until the onion is soft, then add the liver. Cook the liver lightly. Stir in the warm boiled rice with the finely chopped parsley. Garlic is meant to be good for keeping worms at bay; however, it is still best to properly worm your dog at regular intervals. Parsley is believed to be good for your dog's liver.

Italian macaroni

INGREDIENTS

2 oz/60g macaroni or other pasta
2 lb/1 kg stewing steak, chopped
oil
1 onion, peeled and grated
3 garlic cloves, sliced
leftover or cooked mixed vegetables
sliced bread or dried kibble

METHOD

Cook the macaroni or other pasta while dicing the steak. Cook the steak for 5 minutes in hot oil with the onion and the garlic. Add the cooked vegetables. Remove and strain the pasta, mix it with the cooked meat and serve. A very quick and easy dish.

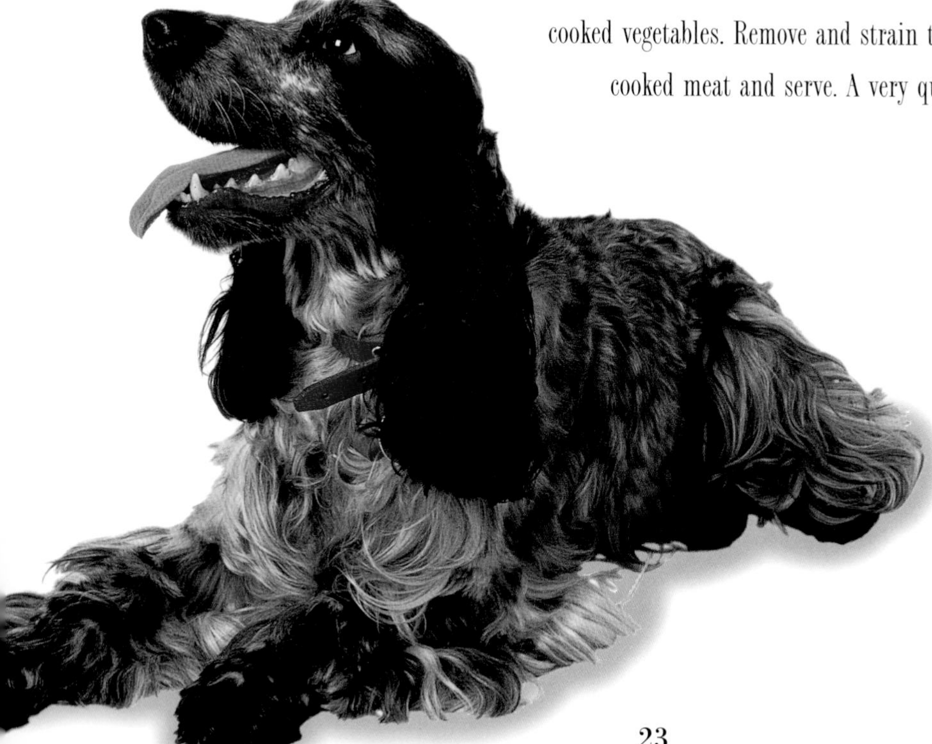

Tuki's favorite pilaf

INGREDIENTS

2 lb/1 kg stewing steak, cubed
1 piece of liver (lamb or beef), chopped into same size cubes as the beef
1 tablespoon olive oil
1 onion, grated
3 cloves garlic, chopped finely
2 chicken stock cubes
2 potatoes, grated
2 carrots, grated
1 piece of pumpkin, 2 inches/6 cm square, grated or diced
2 zucchini, grated
5 cups water
1/2 cup oatmeal
2 cups brown rice

METHOD

Brown the steak in the oil, then add the liver and brown very lightly. Add the onion and the garlic and stir for a moment. Lower the heat and simmer. Crumble 2 chicken stock cubes into the meat, add potato, carrot, pumpkin and zucchini. Add 5 cups of water, then the oatmeal and rice. Cover and simmer until the rice is cooked. Add more liquid if necessary. (Stock can be used instead of water and stock cubes.)

Healthy weekend bake

INGREDIENTS

2 lb/1 kg lean meat
1 piece of liver (lamb or beef)
vegetables such as potato, pumpkin, zucchini, onion, eggplant, tomato, cabbage (have twice as much vegetables as meat)
5 cloves garlic, chopped
5 cups of water or stock
2 stock cubes
2 cups brown rice or rolled oats

METHOD

Chop the meat and liver. Grate the vegetables you have on hand. Add the chopped garlic, the water or stock, and the stock cubes. Add the brown rice or rolled oats. Cook until the rice or oats are cooked. The stew can be thickened with a little wholewheat flour, cornflour or small pasta.

Substitute chicken or boneless fish for variety.

Note: This is a big weekend bake, to last two dogs for four or five days (depending on their appetites). Refrigerate or freeze.

The stock pot

Whenever fresh chickens or wings or pieces of meat and bones are used for stocks and soups in the kitchen, remove the cooked flesh—minus the bones—before all the goodness has been removed from it and mix it in a big bowl of mashed and cooked vegetables, with cooked rice or pasta and perhaps some of the better dried food for a good healthy meal for your dog.

Chicken stock

Roaster chickens are cheaper, or you can buy bones and carcasses (even cooked ones) from butcher shops. Chop roughly with a cleaver to release the bone marrow juices, add any jellied cooking juices or gravy, cover with cold water in a pot, and simmer for several hours for strong flavors and richness. Strain off the debris, and save all the stock. Jellied stock can be mixed with any meat and grated or cooked vegetables or used with cooked rice.

Fish stock

Keep shrimp shells, fish heads and skeletons in a freezer bag and keep frozen until you have enough saved to make a good stock. Put all the bits into a stock pot with cold water and boil until reduced. Simmer for half an hour, then strain. Any fish flesh can be used for dogs or cats, as long as you have discarded the bones. Stock can be mixed with any meat and grated or cooked vegetables or used with cooked rice.

Minnie's fish head stew

INGREDIENTS

4 lb/2 kg fish heads and bones
2 carrots, finely chopped
2 onions, finely chopped
1 or 2 tomatoes chopped
2 cups cooked rice or pasta
1 lb/500g fish

METHOD

Put the fish heads into a pan with the vegetables and add water to just cover. Bring to a boil. When the fish heads begin to break up, take out and sieve the juice back into the pot. Boil down and use rice or pasta to thicken. Add bits of fish flesh (bones removed) and simmer for a few minutes.

Seared fish

Buy any cheap fish and freeze in plastic bags. The fish can be taken straight out of the freezer and microwaved (in the bag). Then scrape the flesh off the bones and mince well with a fork or in a food processor. Add to a dish of well-cooked rice or pasta.

Kanine kedgeree

INGREDIENTS

1 lb/500g boneless fish
milk and water
1 onion, peeled
2 tablespoons oil
1 lb/500g rice, cooked until soft
3 or 4 hard-boiled eggs, chopped
carrot, grated
parsley, chopped

METHOD

Put the fish in a pan, cover with a mixture of half milk and half water, simmer for 20 minutes. Lift the fish out and flake the flesh. Chop and fry the onion in the oil, stir in the cooked rice, the fish and the chopped eggs. Add grated carrot and chopped parsley.

Cassoulet

INGREDIENTS

1 lb/500g steak, diced
125g (4 oz) ground beef
2 cloves garlic, sliced
2 onions, chopped
1 cup cabbage, chopped
1 cup carrots, diced
1 cup beans, sliced

METHOD

Brown the garlic and the onion in a little oil, add the meats and stir until heated. Add 1 tablespoon of water and cover. Simmer for half an hour, stirring often and adding more water to stop it drying out. Stir in the vegetables and cook for a few more minutes.

Stuffed heart

INGREDIENTS

1 ox heart
milk
breadcrumbs
2 cloves garlic, chopped
1 cup rice, cooked until soft
2 tablespoons oil or fat
1 cup water
vegetables (such as carrots, turnips, potatoes pumpkin etc), finely grated

METHOD

Heart is not tender, but dogs (and cats) enjoy it. Rinse the heart, slit it open on one side, cut out the big membranes and veins, rinse and drain. The old-fashioned method was then to soak the heart in buttermilk, but try soaking it in milk. Fill the cavity with bread crumbs, chopped garlic and half the cooked rice, tie the heart back together with string, then brown it in the oil and any leftover bacon bits and fat. Put it in an oven dish with the water and vegetables around it. Cover tightly and simmer for nearly 2 hours. The heart can be carved into slices and served with the vegetables and the remaining rice mixed in the juices.

Stir-fry

A quick way to use leftover boiled rice

INGREDIENTS

1 tablespoon safflower oil
1 onion, finely grated
2 cloves garlic, finely sliced
1 lb/500g ground beef
2 eggs, beaten lightly
4 or 5 cups boiled rice
dash of soy sauce

METHOD

Heat the wok, pour in the oil and swirl it around. Put in the onion and garlic, then the beef. Toss until browned. Pour in the beaten eggs, then the boiled rice and toss, to coat the rice with the beef. Add the soy sauce. This can be reheated in the microwave to room temperature after being stored in the refrigerator.

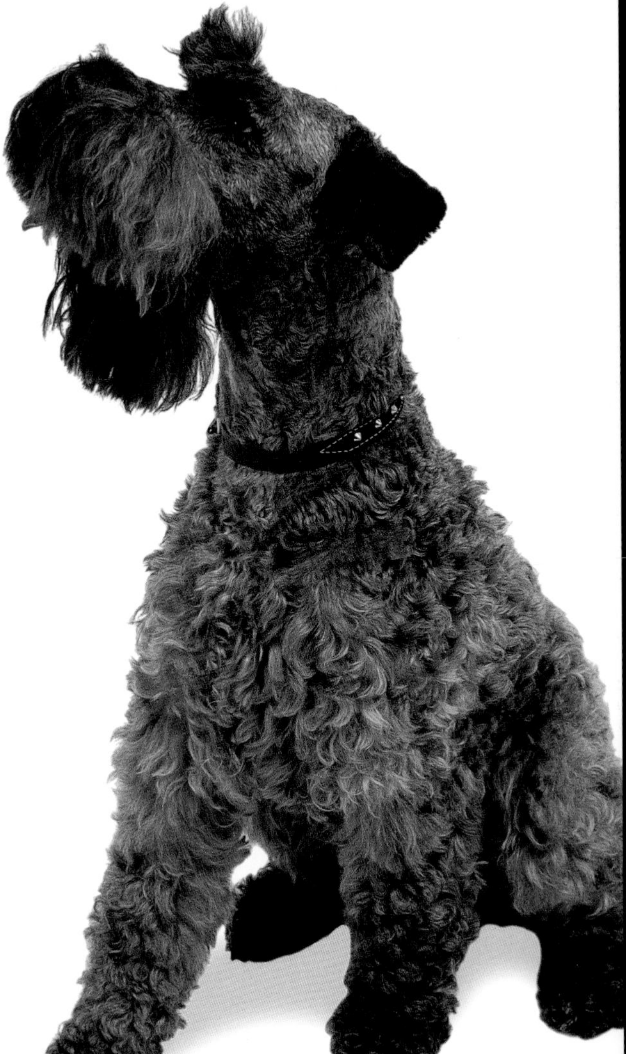

Chicken aspic

INGREDIENTS

1 lb/500g chicken wings
2 cloves of garlic, peeled
1 onion
1 stalk of celery
a handful of green beans
water

METHOD

This is the sort of food you cook while you are busy doing something else. Put the chicken wings into a pot and add enough water to cover. Coarsely chop the garlic, onion, celery and beans and add to the pot. Simmer for about 20-30 minutes. Remove the chicken wings and vegetables from the water and remove all the meat from the chicken bones. Chop the meat. Set the meat and vegetables aside and put the bones back into the pot of water. Simmer for about two hours. Discard the bones and return the reserved meat and vegetables to the stock. Refrigerate until set.